Thirsty, Thirsty
Elephants

For grandmothers everywhere!—S. M.

For Irina and her many grandmothers,
past and present.—F. V.

Text copyright © 2017 by Sandra Markle
Illustrations copyright © 2017 by Fabricio VandenBroeck
All rights reserved, including the right of reproduction in whole or in part in any form.
Charlesbridge and colophon are registered trademarks of Charlesbridge Publishing, Inc.

Published by Charlesbridge
85 Main Street
Watertown, MA 02472
(617) 926-0329
www.charlesbridge.com

Library of Congress Cataloging-in-Publication Data
Markle, Sandra, author.
    Thirsty, thirsty elephants / Sandra Markle; illustrated by Fabricio VandenBroeck.
        pages cm
    ISBN 978-1-58089-634-4 (reinforced for library use)
    ISBN 978-1-60734-840-5 (ebook)
    ISBN 978-1-60734-841-2 (ebook pdf)
1. African elephant—Juvenile literature. 2. Droughts—Tanzania—Juvenile literature.
I. VandenBroeck, Fabricio, 1954– illustrator. II. Title.
QL737.P98M3694 2016
599.67'4—dc23   2015017345

Printed in China
(hc) 10 9 8 7 6 5 4 3 2 1

Illustrations done in acrylics and watercolors on a custom texturized paper
    and then manipulated in Photoshop
Display type set in Museo by Jos Buivenga
Text type set in Museo Slab by Jos Buivenga
Color separations by Colourscan Print Company Pte Ltd, Singapore
Printed by 1010 Printing International Limited in Huizhou, Guangdong, China
Production supervision by Brian G. Walker
Designed by Martha MacLeod Sikkema

Thirsty, Thirsty
Elephants

Sandra Markle

Illustrated by Fabricio VandenBroeck

ⓘ Charlesbridge

It's a hot, dry day in Tanzania. Grandma elephant stops munching leaves. Thirsty, she lifts her trunk high and takes a deep *SNIFF!*

Grandma smells water in the distance and sets off. Mother elephant comes last, with Little Calf holding tight to her tail.

Grandma leads the way through the rosy glow of the fading day. When the herd reaches the river, the bank is already crowded with gazelles, zebras, and giraffes. But the other animals move aside for the elephants.

Grandma sucks in a trunkful of water and shoots this
big drink down her throat. Little Calf fills up her trunk, too.
She blows the water out but misses her mouth and sprays
Grandma. Grandma presses her trunk on the baby's back.
Little Calf kneels and drinks through her mouth. *GULP!*

Another dry day follows. There have been many in this long drought. Grandma keeps the herd close to the river. But each day, the water level drops.

Finally, there's barely enough for the gazelles, zebras, and giraffes.

There's not enough for the elephants.

Grandma leads the search for another watering hole.
The one they find is dry. Grandma digs her tusks into
the ground.

Mother and the other adults dig, too. Slowly, a little water seeps into the holes. The entire herd takes a **SLURP**.

But there's not enough for the elephants.

Grandma's thirst stirs a memory of a dry time long ago,
when she was a baby like Little Calf. She remembers another
watering hole and sets off to find it. On the way, the herd stops
in a thicket to munch leaves.

Little Calf chews and chomps. There is juice in each **CRUNCH!**
But it's not nearly enough for the thirsty elephants.

Grandma leads the herd on. From time to time, she sniffs for the scent of the watering hole. Mother and the others sniff, too. Little Calf sniffs once. She gets a trunkful of dust. *KACHOO!*

When Grandma smells water, she holds her trunk high to track the scent. Soon the rest of the herd smells water, too. They charge to find it. But the water is deep down in a well. Out of reach.

There's not a drop for the thirsty elephants.

On and on the herd trudges, following Grandma across the dry land. Little Calf gets so hot she drops. Mother bends her trunk into her own mouth and sucks up some saliva. She sprays her baby. *SWOOSH!* This cools Little Calf just enough.

When Little Calf gets up, Mother and the others keep her in their shadows. The hot, hot sun beats down. The thirsty, thirsty elephants walk on, slowly. Grandma finally smells what she's been searching for.

She trumpets for the herd. Mother and the others hurry.
Little Calf trots as fast as she can. Grandma leads them to . . .

At last, there is enough.

Little Calf sucks up a trunkful and squirts it into her mouth. She drinks her fill. Then, watching Grandma and Mother shower, Little Calf copies them. She misses and sprays Grandma. *SPLASH!*

Grandma sprays Little Calf right back. They play until the sun sets. Then Grandma and Little Calf sink down for a soak. Grandma remembers this place from a thirsty, thirsty time long ago.

Now, Little Calf will remember it, too.

Author's Note

There's very often a real animal that inspires each of my books. This book is based on the story of an older elephant that saved her herd during a long drought. Researchers named her Big Mama.

It happened in 1994, when a drought that struck the Tarangire National Park area of Tanzania went on for several years. Finding a source of water close to food was becoming impossible, as all kinds of grazers packed together on the banks of the park's shrinking rivers. Many different kinds of animals were drinking up the diminishing rivers and eating all the grass. It became harder and harder for herds of elephants to get the nourishment that they need in order to stay healthy.

However, this wasn't the first time the area had suffered such a long drought. A shortage of water had also happened about thirty years earlier. In the wild, elephants can live well into their late sixties. Dr. Charles Foley, a researcher with the Wildlife Conservation Society in Tanzania, was interested in the behavior of an elephant that had lived through both droughts. This elephant was Big Mama. Dr. Foley believes that when water became scarce in 1994, Big Mama led her herd away from their familiar grazing area to new water sources that she might have remembered visiting during the earlier drought, when she was just a calf.

Dr. Foley said, "The elephants aren't radio-collared, so I don't know exactly where Big Mama took her herd. However, after the rains came and her herd returned to the park, they were in good condition, unlike some herds led by much younger females. I believe Big Mama led her herd to a water source she remembered from that earlier drought."

I'm delighted to share that, as of 2016, Big Mama is still alive and her herd is now forty elephants strong—the second largest in Tarangire National Park in Tanzania.

Amazing Elephant Facts

- Elephant calves take about twenty-two months to develop before they are born. At birth, a baby elephant already weighs around 250 pounds (113 kilograms). Usually the baby is standing and walking in less than an hour.
- Elephants eat plants. Depending on its size, an elephant needs between 220 and 440 pounds (100 and 220 kilograms) of food each day. Elephants are grazers and feed on grasses, leaves, fruit, and bark.
- Depending on its size, an elephant's trunk can hold between 4 and 8 gallons (15 and 30 liters) of water at a time. Elephants cannot drink through their trunks. They use their trunks to shoot water down their throats or to shower themselves. On average, an adult elephant drinks about 50 gallons (189 liters) of water a day but usually not all at one time. To stay healthy, an elephant cannot go more than a couple of days without water.
- An elephant can lift its trunk above its head to pick up scents, including the smell of water several miles/kilometers away.
- An elephant's wrinkled skin helps keep its large body from drying out. Water evaporates more slowly between the skin's wrinkles than it would if the elephant's skin were smooth. To protect its skin, an elephant rolls in mud or dusts itself with dirt. The skin's wrinkles hold on to the dirt, forming a shield against the sun's burning rays and against insect bites.

Acknowledgments

Thank you to Dr. Charles Foley of the Wildlife Conservation Society in Tanzania for sharing his time, expertise, and enthusiasm for Africa's elephants. A special thank-you to Skip Jeffery, for his loving support during the creative process.

Digging Deeper

To discover more about African elephants, check out these books and websites:

Joubert, Beverly and Dereck. *Face to Face with Elephants.* Face to Face with Animals. Washington, DC: National Geographic Children's Books, 2008.
Stunning photographs take you along with noted wildlife writer Dereck Joubert as he studies elephants that face threats from lions and from people.

O'Connell, Caitlin, and Donna M. Jackson. *The Elephant Scientist.* Scientists in the Field. Boston, MA: Houghton Mifflin Books for Children, 2011.
Caitlin O'Connell has spent nineteen years studying elephants in the wild. Read about how she surveys elephants in Africa and makes amazing discoveries.

African Elephants (www.africanelephants.com)
Explore this photo-rich site and learn about current research projects.

BBC Nature Wildlife: African elephants (www.bbc.co.uk/nature/life/African_elephant)
Learn about African elephant behavior and see a map of where most elephants live in Africa. Click on "See all African elephants news stories" to investigate elephant behavior.

The Wildlife Conservation Society (www.wcstanzania.org)
Along with elephants, discover several other critically endangered species in Tanzania that WCS works to protect.

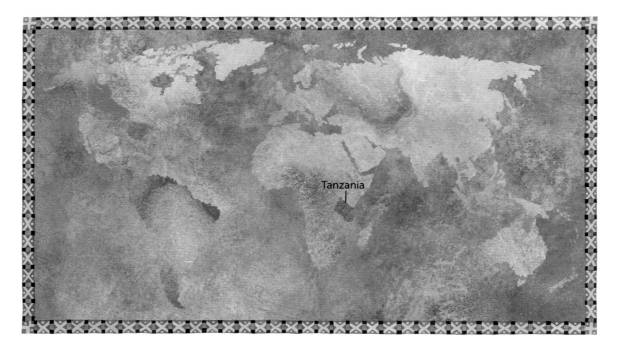